Stoney Point Climber's Guide

by
Christopher Owen

ISBN 0-9654448-0-5

Table of Contents

~ DEDICATION ~

To N my wife, and companion.

PREFACE (1st EDITION)

A lot of people climb at Stoney Point, some may not welcome this publication, mainly because it will be perceived as a precursor to a mass invasion, and ultimately the destruction of this area.
Obviously, this is not the purpose of this book. This book is dedicated to the spirit of conserving the rock, and the environment. The times are changing, climbing is changing, many new people are coming to the sport and needless to say all are welcome, the purpose of this book is to preserve and maintain the traditional aspects of climbing at Stoney Point and to encourage all who climb to love and protect the rock.

C.O. July 1994.

PREFACE (2nd EDITION)

Some things have changed at Stoney Point; bolts have appeared, a sign and notice board have appeared, holds have broken off and climbs have got harder. The main change for this edition has been the inclusion of some boulder problems close to the top-rope climbs, one can enjoy these while friends are dangling. The graffiti still piles up, streak upon streak, the styles of today obliterating the styles of yesteryear. I would urge anyone who frequents Stoney Point to contact the city and attempt to make their opinions known, it may make a difference.

C.O. May 1997.

DISCLAIMER...
Climbing is dangerous! Therefore, climb at your own risk. It is your responsibility to safeguard yourself, no responsibility is assumed by the author of this book for the personal safety of others. Route descriptions are no substitute for experience, it is your responsibility to teach yourself to climb safely.

Wednesday

We are joined at the hip,
and not terminally hip.
We seek not approval
and of ourselves do not approve.
But we dance.
Shades adorning
and motion forming, we dance.
Not to demonstrate.
Not to masturbate.
But to feel and look
into eyes of Siamese twins
joined at the heart.
On a grain of salt watered stone,
in a corner of a darkened room
we swoon.
As we feel the element of success
we suspend ourselves
and shout to clouds
bloodied at day's end;
so disaffected.
We return and laugh
and know the look
in the eyes of men.
So we drink and criticize
and consider ourselves
so, so above it all;
people look at us as we leave
and wonder at what was missed...
Wednesday.

A table of comparative international grades

USA	Vermin	French	British
5.7		5	4c
5.8		5+	5a
5.9		6a	
5.10a	V0	6a+	5b
5.10b			
5.10c	V0+	6b	5c
5.10d		6b+	
5.11a	V1	6c	
5.11b	V2	6c+	6a
5.11c		7a	
5.11d	V3	7a+	
5.12a	V4	7b	6b
5.12b	V5	7b+	
5.12c			
5.12d	V6	7c	6c
5.13a	V7	7c+	
5.13b	V8	8a	7a
5.13c		8a+	
5.13d	V9	8b	
5.14a	V10	8b+	7b
5.14b			

QUALITY RATING SYSTEM
*** Stoney Classic.
** A very good climb.
* A better than average climb.

The route lengths are approximations!

TRASH

Let's face it, Stoney Point is trashed. Please try to take out some trash whilst you are here and discourage people from being untidy (climbers included). Try to help if there are any clean up activities being held.

GRAFFITI

The graffiti is getting worse, and it needs to be cleaned off not painted over, I urge everyone reading this book to write to City Hall and make their views known. There is currently an underground movement to get something done about this and any constructive commentary would be welcome, either to me or City Hall.

STONEY POINT RACK

The following equipment will enable any climb to be top-roped:-

Two 50ft lengths of 1" webbing
Two 20ft lengths of 1" webbing
A small selection of sewn slings for fine tuning
Five locking carabiners
#6-#10 Hexentrics
Set of Friends or equivalent
Two 3/8" bolt hangers with nuts (3/8" & 1/4")

CREEPY CRAWLIES etc..

The nearest emergency room is at *Northridge Medical Center*.
The 2 main nasties here are Poison Oak and Rattlers...
There is a lot of Poison Oak on the north side, learn to recognize it; a group of 3 slick shiny leaves gives it away - don't touch it! If you do you'll get a rash a few days later, use Caladryl or take hot baths to get relief, if it doesn't get any better go see a doctor. This stuff spreads so wash all of your clothes etc..
If you get bitten by a snake, *relax*. Walk to your car and go to the emergency room. They'll pump you full of horse serum and you'll be in hospital for at least a few days for observation.

CORRESPONDENCE

Information or comments can be sent to SOWR@earthlink.net
or visit the Urban Rock Web Site at: http://home.earthlink.net/~sowr

ACKNOWLEDGEMENTS

I would like to thank the following people for their help and companionship in the creation of this work: Antonio Avitia, Fred Batliner, Raymond Bowen, Jonathan Bowman, Marc Burns, Marc Chrysanthou, Norah Flynn, Noreen Flynn, John Fujii, Mark Goss, Brad Kahn, Steve Kahan, Charly Lai, Tony Morino, Mike Newheart, Joe O'Connor, Chris Savage, Tony Tennessee, Mark Torabayashi, Terry Wasson-Graf, Melody Wong, Ralph Wronker II.

stoney point

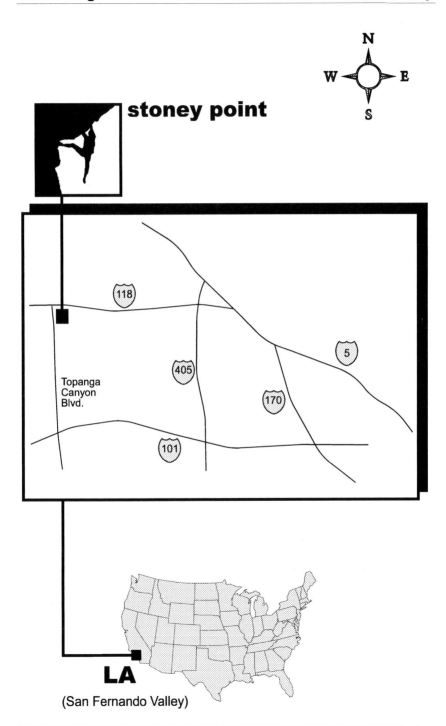

N
W E
S

118

405

5

170

Topanga
Canyon
Blvd.

101

LA
(San Fernando Valley)

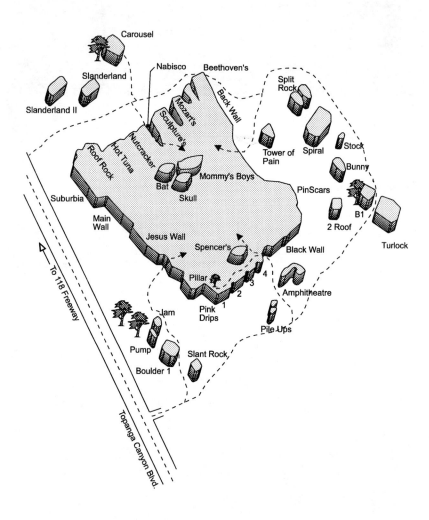

Carousel

Nabisco   Beethoven's

Slanderland

Split
Rock

Slanderland II

Mozart's
Sculpture

Back Wall

Tower of   Spiral   Stock
Pain

Nutcracker

Roof Rock

Hot Tuna

Bunny

Mommy's Boys

Bat   Skull

PinScars

Suburbia

B1

Main
Wall

2 Roof

Jesus Wall

Spencer's

Black Wall

Turlock

Pillar

Amphitheatre

To 118 Freeway

Jam

Pink
Drips

Pile Ups

Pump

Slant Rock

Boulder 1

Topanga Canyon Blvd.

THE
ROUTES

Possible
Leads
p 16 /1
17/6
19/1
22/-
23/∂

'He swung up rock with a long thigh, a lifted knee and
a ripple of irresistible movement. A perfect physique
and a pursuing mind came together.'

G.W.Young on George Mallory

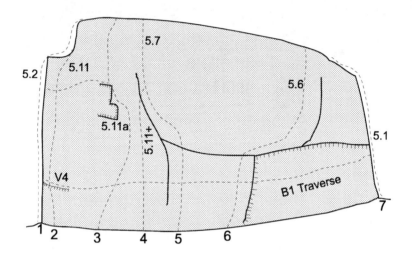

Boulder 1 ~ West Side

The traditional meeting place. Although the east side of this boulder is usually done unroped, the west side is a little taller and a top rope can be helpful especially for beginners. The top of the boulder can be reached by climbing East Face Route; bolts and nuts make up the anchor. Route length 25'.

1. **WEST FACE**** 5.2. The arete is steep, yet has good holds.
2. **NYLON BOY*** 5.11. A line of flakes leads up the wall to the left of Boot Flake.
3. **BOOT FLAKE**** 5.11a. The crux is reaching the flake, although the moves above are not easy.
4. **ENDO BOY*** 5.11+. Very small incut holds lead to Short Story.
5. **SHORT STORY**** 5.7. Getting past the sloping ledge near the top is the crux.
6. **VIVARIN*** 5.6. After gaining a ledge step right. The wall above is the crux.
7. **EAST FACE ROUTE*** 5.1. A tough start leads to better holds.

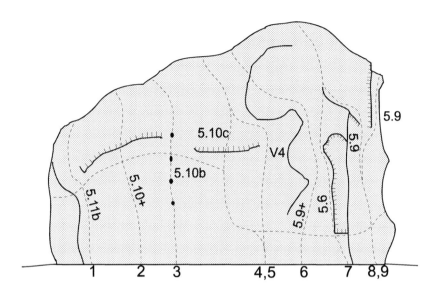

Boulder 1 ~ East Side.
A rather large social scene can be experienced here on a summer's eve. A fellow boulderer once told me that he came here to climb one evening and spent 2 hours talking! Generally speaking the problems are hard, with polished holds, if you prefer a more secluded spot try the north face traverses.

B1 TRAVERSE* V4. North and south are rest areas, the remainder is mostly steep and fingery, especially the NW corner if you stay low.
1. **SE CORNER** 5.11b. The start is very balancy, the head straight up. As a variation it's possible to go right along the undercling.
2. **10-40** 5.10+. A reachy start leads to the undercling, going over this requires nerve.
3. **THREE PIGS*** 5.10b. "Your 1st 5.10". The pinscars are only good when you pull sideways. As a variation ignore the pinscars...5.11b.
4. **UNDERCLING** 5.10c. Reach the undercling via weird moves. A chopped hold up and right might give you courage to go. A variation (Yabo Mantle 5.11+) eliminates the chopped hold.
5. **VAINO'S DYNO**** V5. How many people do you see doing a 2 handed dyno?
6. **NOSE ELIMINATE**** 5.9+. Reachy at the start, head straight up on small holds.
7. **THE NOSE*** 5.6. Either lieback it or come up from the right, then climb up the slab.
8. **DIHEDRAL LEFT** 5.9. A tough mantel onto the ledge on the left.
9. **DIHEDRAL RIGHT** 5.9. An even tougher move to gain the righthand ledge.

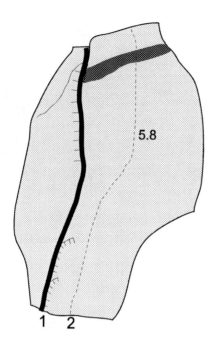

Jam Rock.
On the north side is a good beginner's jam crack. Get to the top by using the East
Face. Slings are good for the anchor. Route length 20'.

1. **THE JAM CRACK*** 5.2. Try this without using holds on the side.
2. **THE FACE*** 5.8. Up the face using side pulls and over the little roof.
3. **CRANKING QUEENIE**** V3. In a cave beneath the Jam Crack; an overhang
problem on not so big holds. Scene of a fatality some years back. *Use a spotter.*

Pump Rock.
Just north of Boulder 1, on the left of the corridor leading to Jam Rock.

1. **THE PUMP TRAVERSE**** 5.11a. If you're tall it's tougher, start off on the left
about an inch from the ground and work your way up and right. Turn the last corner and mantle up, try not to break a rib.

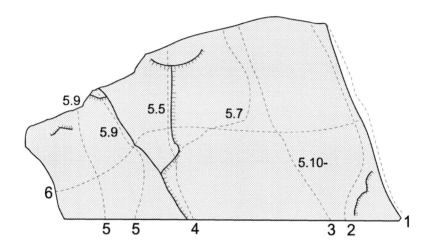

Slant Rock.

1. **THE SLAB*** 5.0. Graded for using hands, try it without.
2. **THE EDGE** 5.2. This is fun no-handed.
3. **NORTH SIDE RH*** 5.10-. Thin edging and smearing to a mantle.
4. **NORTH SIDE LH** 5.5. Large flakes. Or go right and up the face, 5.7.
5. **MANTLES** 5.9. The right hand one is a little harder.
6. **TRAVERSE*** 5.11+. From left to right is a lot harder than the other way and involves a blind side-dyno (!).

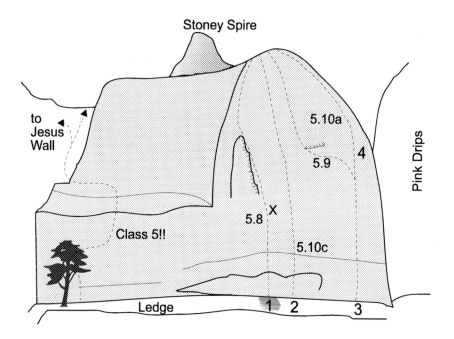

Stoney Spire

to Jesus Wall

5.10a

5.9

4

Pink Drips

5.8 X

Class 5!!

5.10c

Ledge   1 2   3

The Pillar.
This buttress is located to the left of Pink Drips. Four climbs can be done using one anchor, which consists of two rivets (take wires) and cam placements or a long, long sling over the pinnacle (Stoney Spire) behind the buttress. Route length 45'.
The top is gained by climbing up the broken buttress which forms an abutment between the Jesus Wall and The Pillar. Head up a steep tricky little wall then traverse right to Stoney Spire.

1. **THE CRACK** 5.8. The crux is stepping left past the bolt; use the flake above with great care. Lead it if you dare.
2. **MANTLEPEACE*** 5.10c. A nasty mantle leads to a steep face.
3. **PILLAR LEFT*** 5.9. Up loose holds then left over an overlap.
4. **PILLAR RIGHT*** 5.10a. Go right then teeter up a slab.
5. **CHATSWORTH CHIMNEY** 5.7. This is located between The Pillar and Pink Drips Wall. Up the chimney then go right and up a trough to finish on top of Pink Drips. Can be led.

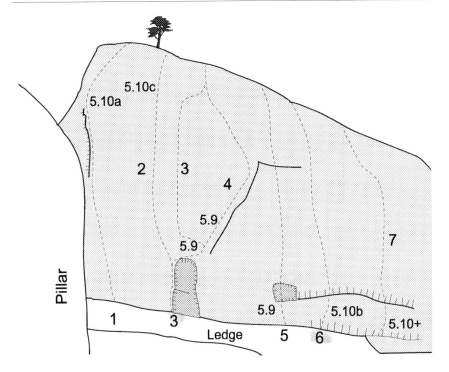

Pink Drips Wall.
This wall features really good steep face climbing of varying difficulty as well as some overhang problems on the right. Use the tree on top for an anchor. Cams will be useful for back up.
Approach is by a ledge which runs past the bottom of Spencer's Slab and above the South Buttresses. Route length 50'.

1. **LEFT ARETE*** 5.10a. Climb just to the right of Chatsworth Chimney, lay off a right facing rib and finish up a fingery wall.
2. **DIRECT**** 5.10b/c. This lies immediately left of Pink Drips, finish straight up using small but positive holds.
3. **PINK DRIPS***** 5.9. A classic face climb; stepping left at the beginning is the crux but don't underestimate the worrying finish.
4. **RIGHT-HAND ROUTE*** 5.9. Instead of going left head up the shallow depression and finish with Pink Drips.
5. **THE BRACKET*** 5.9. A nose of rock sticks out of the face, get on top of it then head straight up. Or pass it on the left.
6. **UNDERWORLD**** 5.10b. Dynos lead to a wall with a deep pocket, the crux is gaining the small ledge above.
7. **WOUNDED KNEE**** 5.10d. Gain a sloping ledge; a real puzzler, step left into a depression then climb the wall above. Both of these climbs end on an easy angled section before the top.

PINK DRIPS 5.9.   *Photo by C.Owen*
The classic Stoney face climb.
John Fujii climbing.

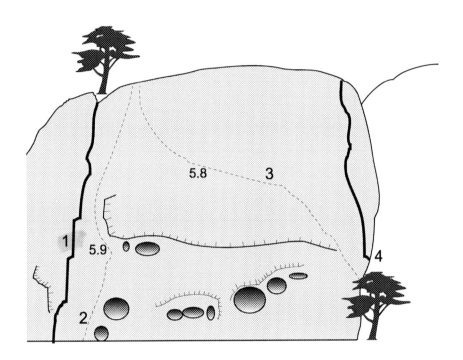

Lower Tier.

This is the wall below The Pillar. It features two crack climbs and two face climbs. These routes end where The Pillar routes start. Use tricky cam placements for the anchor set up or use the anchor on The Pillar and combine them with those routes. Route length 35'.

1. **FLAKY CRACK*** 5.7. This crack can be led.
2. **TIERDROP*** 5.9. Climb right of the crack up some interesting, if a little loose, overlaps.
3. **SLAB ROUTE** 5.8. Start up the right edge then head up and left over a slab.
4. **RIGHT-HAND CRACK** 5.8. Gain the crack from the right edge and follow it to the ledge. A little loose.

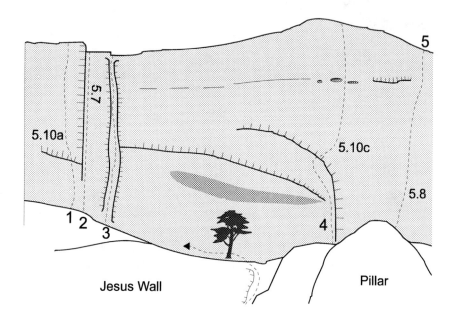

Upper Tier.
Above The Pillar there is a wall with some arches on its left side, this is the Upper Tier. To reach the top, either climb up the broken buttress to the right of The Jesus Wall, then up and left over ledges, or go around the south side of Stoney Point and head up past Spencer's Slab. Nuts and long slings provide the anchors. Route length 30'/40'.

1. **POCKET ROCKET*** 5.10a. Up the overhanging wall using pockets.
2. **CROWN OF THORNS**** 5.7. Short but sweet. Gain the obvious open book then lieback to the top finishing with a tricky mantle move.
3. **ARCH CHIMNEY** 5.5.   The weakness to the right of Crown of Thorns.
4. **RAINBOW'S END**** 5.10+. A very exposed climb, use the pin scarred crack to get over the overlap. The crux is climbing the very steep wall above.
5. **STUDLEY SLAB** 5.8. This takes the face with the bolt studs in it.

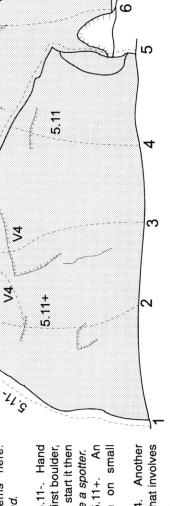

Pile Ups aka Angel's Wings

On the left hand side of the trail when walking towards Turlock. Turn left here to find the Amphitheatre also. There's some tough boulder problems here. *Hard landing, use a pad.*

1. LIP TRAVERSE** 5.11-. Hand traverse the lip of the first boulder, technically tough at the start it then becomes a pump. *Use a spotter.*

2. PILE DRIVER** 5.11+. An overhanging problem on small holds.

3. PILE LIEBACK* V4. Another overhanging problem that involves a lunge from a lieback.

4. SLEDGEHAMMER* 5.11+. More overhanging hardness.
5. PILE UP MANTLE 5.11. Mantle up on the end of the boulder.
6. S. FACE 5.11. Even more overhanging hardness.
7. E. FACE** 5.10+. Thin edging and smearing then around the corner and up.
8. EASY ROUTE* 5.8. Climb up the face using the pocket, or eliminate the pocket for a tougher (5.10) problem.

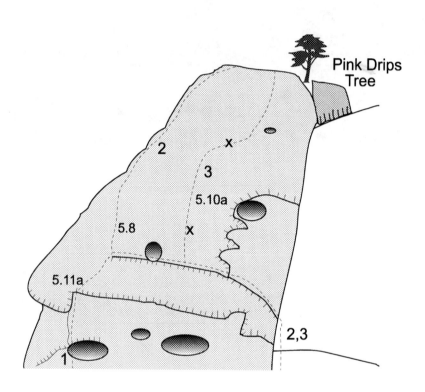

Buttress #1.
This buttress is actually the right hand edge of the Pink Drips Wall. Use the Pink Drips tree for an anchor. It may also be possible to use some nuts/cams in the cracks by the chockstone. Route length 50'.

1. **BATMAN AND OWEN*** 5.11a. Another overhang. Gain the niche below a roof, pull over the roof using finger pockets and follow the easier arete to the top.
2. **THE RIDDLER**** 5.8. Gain the same arete by traversing in from the chimney to the right. The crux is a mantle on to a knob.
3. **BOLTED LEAD** 5.10a. Follow the bolts up the face to the right of the arete.
4. **CHOCKSTONE CHIMNEY** 5.5. The nasty chimney up past the chockstone.

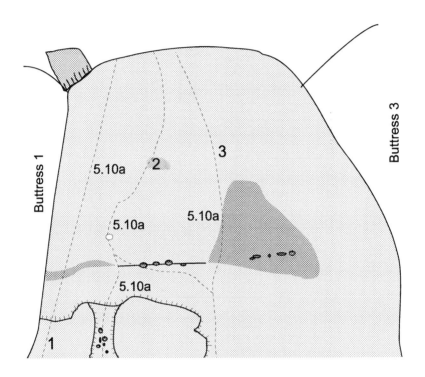

Buttress #2.

Some of the better slab climbs at Stoney are located on this buttress. The Pink Drips tree and nuts/cams make up the anchor. Take care not to get the rope snagged on an expansion bolt sleeve sticking out of the slab near the top. Route length 40'.

1. **CHOCKSTONE WALL** 5.10a. A line can be found to the right of the chimney.
2. **MUGNESEA LUNG**** 5.10a. Once upon a time this route was a lead, the bolts are widely spaced and very bad, it's best to TR. Climb delicately just left of the front of the slab.
3. **SAVAGE SLAB**** 5.10a. Another delicate climb which heads up the front of the slab and eventually joins the left route.
4. **THE SLOT** 5.8. A monster of an offwidth up the forbidding undercut crack.

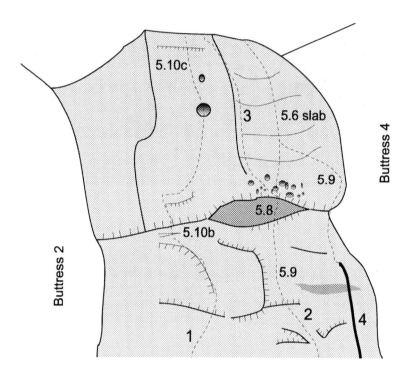

Buttress #3.
The roof routes on this buttress should not be missed. They are both classics. For the anchor sling a boulder and use some nuts/cams in a crack on the right. Route length 45'.

1. **EYE OF FAITH*** 5.10c. A great route. Pull up over the roof and climb up the wall, past "The Eye", to a belly flop finale.
2. **PAUL'S HOLE*** 5.9. The crux is getting up to the overhang. Avoid any temptation to crawl into the hole. Pull and stem over the overhang. The slab above is sheer delight.
3. **CONNECTIONS*** 5.9. It's possible to leave Paul's Hole above the overhang and climb up the faint rib to the right of Eye Of Faith.
4. **NOW VOYAGER** 5.9. This starts at the bottom of Paul's Hole but wanders to the right up over a steep section, then joins the top slab.
5. **NOT ANOTHER ONE** 5.3. Yes, another chimney.

EYE OF FAITH 5.10c.   *Photo by C.Owen*
An Urban Rock classic.
Steve Kahan climbing.

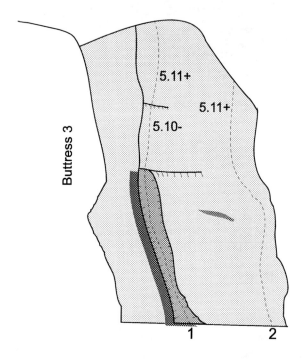

Buttress #4.
This buttress gets steep at the top and the holds all but disappear. A boulder sitting on top provides an anchor. Watch out for broken glass beneath it. Route length 50'.

1. **SEMIDETACHED**** 5.11+. Go up the rib which rests on the buttress, past a tricky step, then up on very small holds (crux). A couple of palmy moves lead to the top.
2. **RIGHT ROUTE** 5.11+. Up a slab, loose, then, when the wall steepens, move to the left (ignoring the chopped holds on the right) and make very thin technical moves to the top.

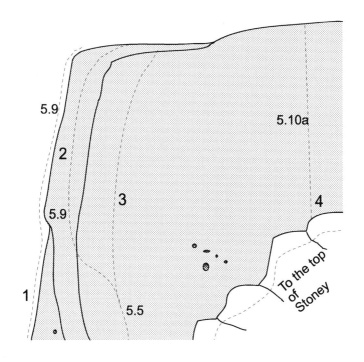

Spencer's Slab.
This is located above Buttress #4 and has an easy slab climb in a good position. Nuts and slings provide an anchor. There are bolt studs too. Route length 35'.

1. **FRONT ROUTE** 5.9. The front pocketed face.
2. **OFFSET SLAB*** 5.10a. Start at the main slab, then go left and climb the subsidiary one.
3. **SPENCER'S SLAB LEFT**** 5.5. A good climb up the left of the slab.
4. **SPENCER'S SLAB RIGHT*** 5.10a. The blank slab on the right.

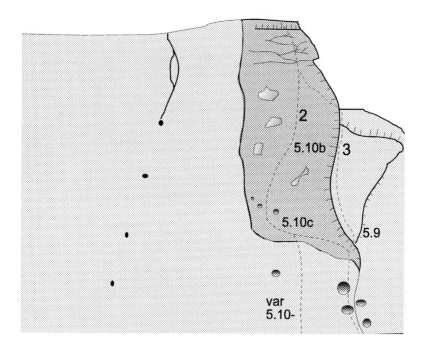

The Black Wall.
This is located to the right of the south side trail to the top of Stoney. Slings, nuts and trees provide an anchor. Route length 35'.

1. **THE BODY CHUTE** 5.7. A dirty flaring crack.
2. **THE BLACK WALL***** 5.10c. The overhanging wall provides an exciting exercise in lock offs and long reaches.
3. **BLACK CRACK*** 5.9. Climb the dihedral to the right of the previous route, then step left and finish up the wall.

These climbs are located below The Black Wall, just above the trail before reaching Turlock:
4. **THE BLACK ROOF*** 5.10b/c. Take the roof crack on the right, get a solid fist jam. The hard part is pulling over the lip.

TODD'S TRAVERSE*** 5.9+. Located in the amphitheater to the left of the previous climb. A boulder traverse at first very balancy and then strenuous. From right to left and back again. 12 times is a 1000ft!

THE BLACK WALL 5.10c.   *Photo by C.Owen*
Great moves on small holds.
Tony Tennessee climbing.

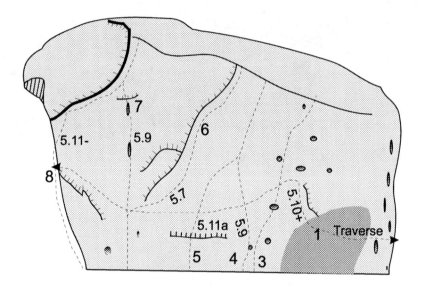

Turlock Front Face.

This boulder is very popular with beginners, justly so, there are some good moderate routes. The eastern overhanging wall is usually bouldered. The bolt anchors on top can be reached by climbing The Stairs.

The routes are described starting at The Stairs and going around clockwise. Route length 25'.

1. **THE BULGE** 5.10+. Start on the right then using a good pocket, reach left, step high; hey this is okay....whoops! This is really the last part of:

2. **TURLOCK TRAVERSE** V5. Start at the stairs, head left. Three of the corners are hard, the back face and the crystal ball section are very hard.

3. **THE STAIRS** 5.0. An easy beginners route using carved holds.

4. **TURLOCK FACE** 5.9. A delicate climb on small holds and smears.

5. **TURLOCK ELIMINATE** 5.11a. A tricky mantle leads to smearing. Ignore the big holds and pockets.

6. **THE FLAKE** *** 5.7. Lieback the flake, a tricky move leads over the top. The flake used to be bigger.

7. **PIN SCARS (AKA SILENT RUNNING)** 5.9. Follow the pin scars, a tough move up and left leads to a depression.

8. **THE CORNER** 5.11-. Lock off on an undercling and, using the arete, head up and left. Strenuous.

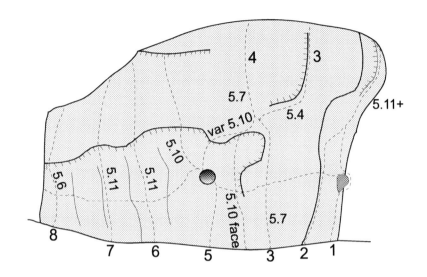

Turlock North Face.

1. **CRYSTAL BALL MANTLE**** 5.11+. An overhanging mantle leads to flakes. The crux is getting over the top.
2. **VARIATION START; CROWD PLEASER**** 5.11. The left edge and flakes lead to the roof. Follow the previous route over the top (5.11+).
3. **NORTH FLAKE*** 5.7. The start is the crux, from the ledge step right and head up the flake.
4. **NORTH FACE*** 5.7. The same start as the previous route, but from the ledge head straight up.

Turlock Back Face.
Stoney's little campus board, in the evening it's in the shade.

5. **HOOF AND MOUTH***** 5.10c. The old yellow book gave it 5.8!. Scrunch yourself up in the pocket, a little more; that's it. Now go up and left for the good jug.
6. **SLIME*** 5.11a. Slick weird holds all rather overhanging lead to the ledge.
7. **PLIERS*** 5.11a. Be quick on this one too.
8. **RAMADA*** 5.6. You too can say that you've done Turlock's Back Face; a small overhang on good holds leads to the slab, head straight up. Major sandbag.

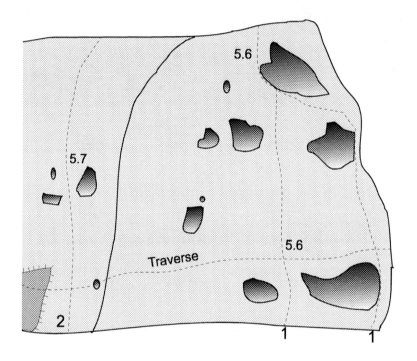

Turlock Pothole Face.

1. **POTHOLES*** 5.6. There are a few variations to this. The crux is usually getting over the top.
2. **UNTOLD STORY*** 5.7. The face left of Potholes is easier to start than it is to finish.

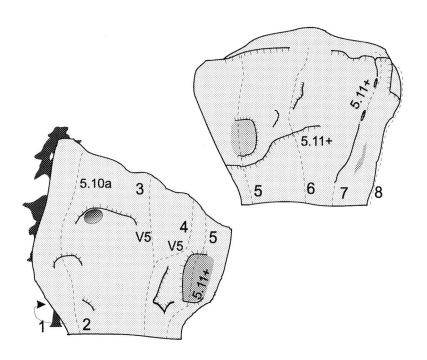

B1 Boulder.
In a word, hardness. Counter clockwise from the tree.

1. **THE CORNER** 5.10a. The 2nd easiest way to the top.
2. **HOG TIED*** 5.10a. The crux is towards the top. *Use a top rope.*
3. **MASTER OF REALITY*** V5. An odd problem using side pulls and pressure, then head straight up!!
4. **EXPANSION CHAMBER**** V5. An odd problem using side pulls and pressure, then head right!!
5. **THE EAR*** 5.11+. Get over the bulge to a recess and wonder why you ever came.
6. **PINK FLOYD*** 5.11+. It's a lot harder without a cheater stone
7. **THE CRACK*** 5.11+. This involves using pockets and dynos, the top move is scary.
8. **THE EDGE*** 5.11+. This smooth face yields (sometimes) to finesse.

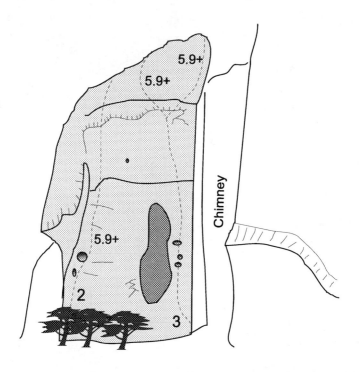

Swiss Cheese Buttress.
This is the pocketed wall to the left of Pin Scars. There are some boulders that can be slung for an anchor behind the top of the buttress. Route length 35'.

1. **PACKER CRACKER** 5.11a. This climb is around the corner to the left. Ascend a curving crack.
2. **LEFT ROUTE** 5.9+. Steep, loose climbing.
3. **RIGHT ROUTE*** 5.9+. Up flakes to a problematical finish either left or right.

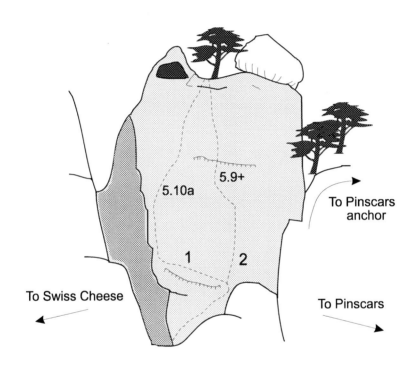

Kitty Litter Slab.
Around the corner to the left of Pin Scars is a slab with a triangular roof on the left at the top. To set up the anchor either go up the gully to the left or reach the top from the Pin Scars anchor. Sling a tree. Route length 35'.

1. **TIDY CAT*** 5.10a. Traverse out to the left edge and smear and palm your way to the top.
2. **JOHNNY CAT*** 5.9+. Head straight up the middle of the slab to a foot pedaling mantle followed by easier climbing.

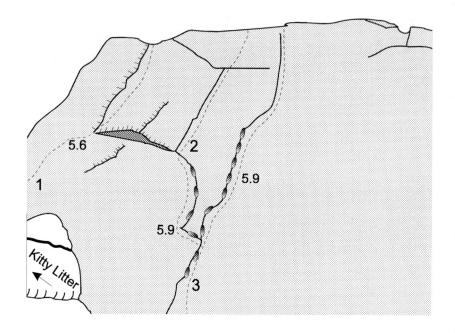

Pin Scars Wall ~ Left Side.
The obvious pin scarred cracks on the wall are visible from the trail near Turlock.
Sling a boulder on top for the anchor. Route length 40'.

1. **SCARFACE*** 5.6. An easy route to the left of the cracks.
2. **MAGNUM CASE*** 5.9. Start at the bottom of the wall and climb up the left hand
pin scarred crack.
3. **PIN SCARS (AKA MACHINE GUN)***** 5.9. The right hand crack proves to be
strenuous. The crux is getting past the steep section.

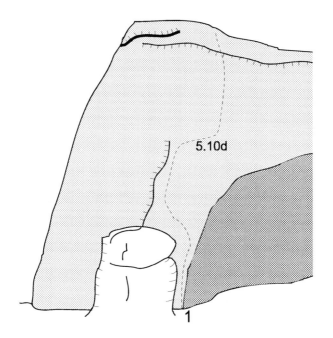

Pin Scars Wall ~ Right Side.

1. **CHANGELING**** 5.10d. This climb is located around the corner to the right.
One dyno after another leads to a ledge. Don't relax though, the crux is next; an
awkward high step leads to better holds and the top.
2. **THE CHIMNEY** 5.5.This is in the corner and is generally soloed.

To the right lie some short walls with 5.9+/5.10 problems. Above and to the left of
these there is a fun lieback crack which is generally bouldered. At the top of the
Pin Scars Wall is a pinnacle which can be soloed.
There is a good view of the city and mountains from here.

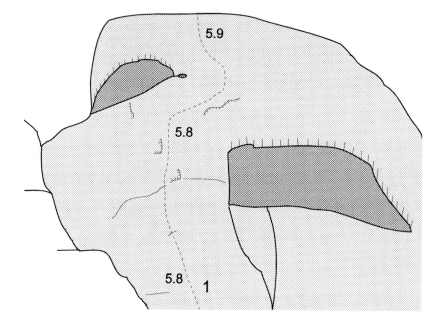

Two Roof Rock.
This is the outcrop above Turlock. It has two roofs with a rib separating them. Use a thread belay at the back of the outcrop. Route length 35'.

1. **RED DAWN*** 5.9+. Climbs up the rib between the roofs. The crux is at the top. Take care with the loose holds in the middle.

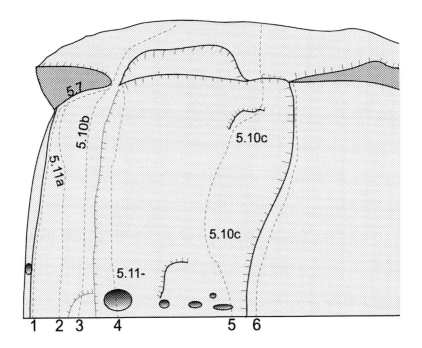

Bunny Rock.
A large outcrop to the left of the trail with an unsavory looking chimney on its right-hand side. Sling and cam the boulder on top. Route length 35'.

1. **OVERHANG PASSBY*** 5.7. Follow the crack to the roof then traverse right; crux, follow another crack to the top.
2. **LAYED OFF*** 5.11a. Thin moves lead to a sloping flake, lay off this to reach a hold way left.
3. **OVERLORD*** 5.10b. Pull over the undercut and follow the wall to a long reach; crux, and then the top.
4. **MIDDLE ROUTE** 5.11-. Tough climbing up the edge. Hard start.
5. **RABBIT'S FOOT*** 5.10c. Climb the overhanging wall just to the left of the chimney. The start is the crux.
6. **RABBIT'S BUTT** ?.??. The must do flaring chimney. Enjoy!

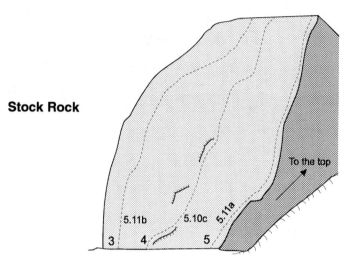

Stock Rock

Stock Rock.
This boulder is in the bushes, just to the left of the trail, before reaching Lions Head. The easiest way up is on the back which is not that easy. Use a thread belay at the back of the boulder, there are also two 1/4" bolt studs on top. Take hangers. Treat the holds with tender loving care! Route length 30".

1. **EASY MONEY** 5.9. Climb up past a large pocket.
2. **BLACK MONDAY*** 5.11+. The blank wall.
3. **BLACK FRIDAY*** 5.11b. Another very fingery climb just to the left of Bull Market.
4. **BULL MARKET*** 5.10c. A difficult start leads to delicate edging.
5. **CORNER THE MARKET**** 5.11a. Lieback tenuously up the arete, using the boulder on the right to step up reduces the grade to 5.9.

Slab Rock.
A large slab just north of Stock Rock, with a large lieback flake on it's south face. Recently uncovered by the "trimmers and mulchers". Boulders and cracks on the top supply adequate anchors.

1. **LIEBACK FLAKE*** 5.7. Boldly lieback up the flake. Pity it's not longer.
2. **PEBBLE TRAVERSE** 5.11b. A finger wearing series of moves on small pockets, pebbles and flakes. Can be connected with the slab traverse.
3. **LEFT SLAB ROUTE*** 5.6. Pull up onto the slab and climb the edge.
4. **THE SLAB**** 5.6. Same start as 3 but head straight up the slab - fun.
5. **SMEDGE**** 5.10a. A tricky mantel leads to very good thin smedging.
6. **COMPOSURE***** 5.9. Another mantel start leads to moves which must be exact or else (especially if you're high ball bouldering!).
7. **RIGHT SLAB ROUTE*** 5.8. After rounding the corner climb up the edge.
8. **SLAB TRAVERSE**** 5.10a. From right to left, balancy and unique for Stoney.

Slab Rock

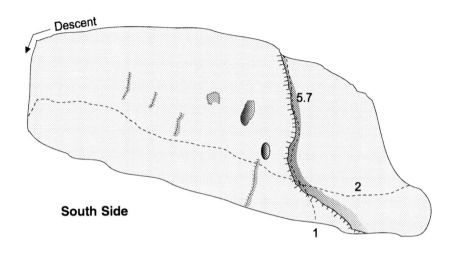

Descent

5.7

2

South Side

1

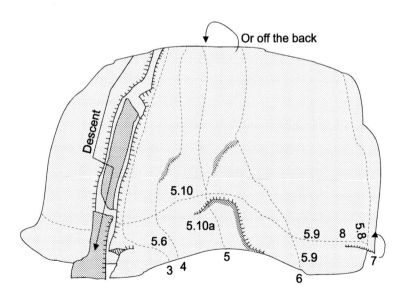

Or off the back

Descent

5.10

5.10a

5.6

5.9   8   5.8

3   4

5

5.9

7

6

East Side

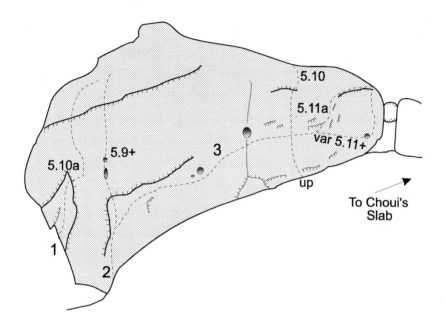

Spiral Boulder ~ West Side.
This is the massive boulder on the left just before reaching Split Rock. Cracks at the bottom of the boulder on the south side provide the anchor. Route length 35'.

1. **AURORA (AKA BOLD DURING)*** 5.10a. Jump for a flake and follow it to a gravel filled depression. Foot pedal to the top.
2. **BOREALIS** 5.9+. Climb up side pulls then a face. The slippery slab leads to the top.
3. **SPIRAL TRAVERSE*** 5.11-. To the right of the top-rope climbs lies this classic boulder traverse, generally it goes from left to right and is very fingery. There are many harder eliminates.

CHOUINARD'S SLAB* 5.9. A thin smearing problem straight up the slab on a boulder just up from the Spiral Traverse.

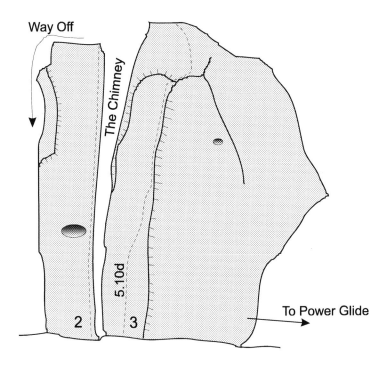

Split Rock.
This formation is cleft by a large chimney, which is recommended as practice for chimneying. For an easy way to the top, climb up the short west face; take slings and nuts for the anchor. Route length 35'.

1. **THE CHIMNEY**** 5.3. Squeeze up into the depths of the chimney; tricky. Then using the classical method head to the top.
2. **ARETE SKELETON** 5.10c. The overhanging arete to the left.
3. **SPLIT DECISION*** 5.10d. A bouldery start leads to an overhanging corner with a crack for thin fingers.

POWER GLIDE** V4. A really strenuous problem which overcomes a little roof and then wall just NE of Split Rock.
EAT OUT MORE OFTEN* 5.11. Traverse right starting at the previous climb. The trees are now in the way.

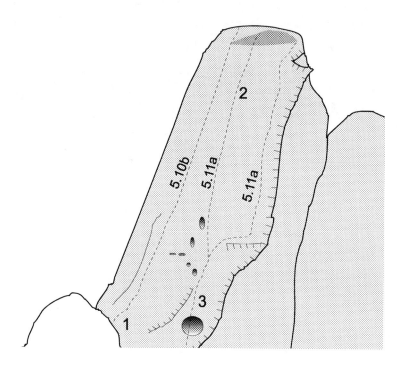

Tower of Pain.
This is the pointed boulder up on the side of the hill before reaching Potholes. There are two good wall climbs on it. Thread a small chockstone at the back for an anchor. Take a hanger. There is also a bolt on top. Be careful, there are some loose holds. Route length 35'.

1. **PREYING MANTIS*** 5.10b. Steep climbing on good holds leads to a delicate crux, follow better holds over the top.
2. **MANTIS MANTEL** 5.11a. Climb straight up between the other two routes, very thin.
3. **CAPTAIN ENERGY*** 5.11a. More good steep climbing to a difficult step right using a hidden pocket. Resting at the ledge proves to be a pump, so head straight up on doubtful holds.

POTHOLES TRAVERSE 5.10+.   *Photo by N.Flynn*
A Back Wall boulder traverse.
Chris Owen climbing.

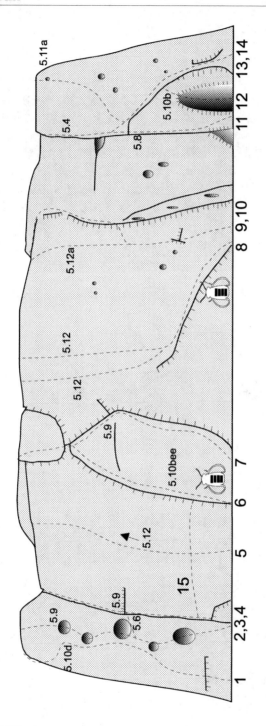

The Back Wall

There's some very steep climbing on this wall, all good stuff, even a couple of moderate routes. Gain the top from either a gully to the left or go up past Beethoven's. The anchors are slung boulders and nut/cam placements; Vicious has a two bolt anchor on top. Route length 35'/40'.

1. **THE WRATH OF KAHAN*** 5.10d. Climb the buttress to the left of Potholes. Some good moves.
2. **POTHOLES**** 5.9. Swing from hole to hole then make a tough move over the bulge. Squirm over the top.
3. **POTHOLES ESCAPE**** 5.7. Follow the potholes, but before reaching the bulge make a committing traverse right into the crack. Thrutch to the top.
4. **POTHOLES CRACK*** 5.9. Jam the crack over the overlap. Can be led.
5. **DART LADY** 5.12. Follow very small holds over the bulge. Recent information suggests that holds may be missing.
6. **A-FRAME LEFT (AKA TARZAN)** 5.10b. Awkward jams and sandy rock make this most strenuous.
7. **A-FRAME RIGHT*** 5.9. A classic crack in a world of faces. Follow the ramp to the right and pull up to the hanging ledge. The crux is leaving this via a tenuous lieback.
8. **THE PLANK** 5.12"bee". Up the ramp, then either left or right up the steep wall above. Only bee keepers need apply.
9. **VICIOUS**** 5.12. Potholes and pin scars lead to a lieback to gain the little pocket. A series of small but positive reinforced holds lead to another pocket. Bouldering moves sometimes lead to the top.
10. **OWL HOLE*** 5.10c. Mortals can head right from the pocket and go up over bulging rock. Finish up the pin scarred corner.
11. **BLACK'S CRACK**** 5.7. An awkward start leads to a strenuous pull onto easier ground. Finish up Beehive.
12. **TELEPHONE BOOTH** 5.10b. A short but strenuous exercise, the crux is pulling over into Beehive.
13. **BEEHIVE***** 5.4. Classic easy climbing up a chimney followed by an exposed corner guaranteed to thrill.
14. **BEEGONE*** 5.11a. Climb the Beehive chimney then step onto the wall using big holds and potholes. These lead to the right edge. The final pothole allows the top to be reached, the crux is making a very strenuous mantle over the top.
15. **POTHOLES TRAVERSE***** 5.10+. From left to right; following the chalked holds proves quite strenuous adding a return, even more so.

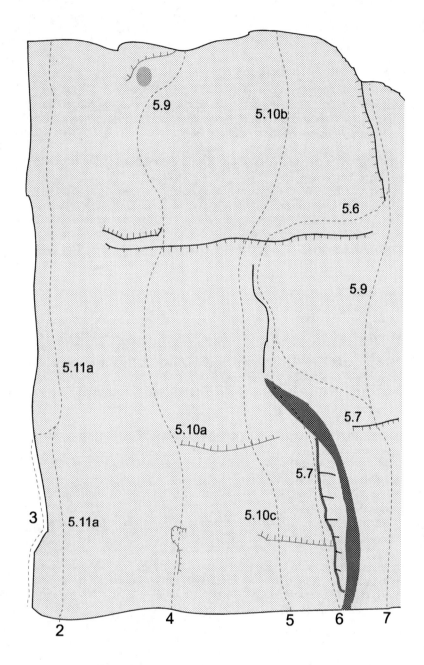

Beethoven's Wall

Beethoven's Wall.
This is the most popular wall at Stoney with good reason:-there are some very good face climbs here. Arrive early to avoid disappointment. The top can be gained by a gully to the right. There are some boulders up there for slings and nuts. Route length 40'.

1. **LEFT EDGE**** 5.11+. Climb up the edge around to the left of The Prow.
2. **THE PROW***** 5.11a. A magnificent climb up the left-hand edge of the wall. The first section is very sustained, either up the edge or, slightly harder, up the face to the right. Continue up the edge to the top.
3. **VARIATION START TO THE PROW**** 5.11a. The mid section can be gained by climbing the wall around the corner to the left and swinging around onto the sloping footholds.
4. **CENTER ROUTE**** 5.10a. This line is just to the right of The Prow. The crux is stepping onto a sloping hold about 10' up, but save some strength for the finish.
5. **DIRECT ROUTE*** 5.10bc. Climb straight up just to the left of the crack. Hard start and hard finish.
6. **BEETHOVEN'S CRACK**** 5.7. A good moderate climb. Up the crack to the ledge, delicately traverse right and finish up another crack.
7. **MANTLE START**** 5.7. Start to the right of the crack, do a mantle move and join the previous route. It is also possible to climb up the steep wall above the mantle, this is 5.9.
8. **DYNOMITE**** 5.12. This climb is located in the approach gully on the righthand side. A tricky start leads to a lieback flake, up this then make a very strenuous and technical traverse right to a pocket. A couple more moves lead to the top.

Canyon Boulder Problems.
Just north of Beethoven's, on either side of the trail. The face to the right is covered in large holds, up the middle is 5.8, the right edge is 5.9.
To the left of the trail;
THE BIRD HOLE* 5.10+. Reach the hole via a lunge from a precarious position - head up wondering why you ever came.
SCRAMBLED EGGS TRAVERSE* 5.11+. Head for the hole from the right, starts out really thin and then becomes a pump, the footholds are invisible.

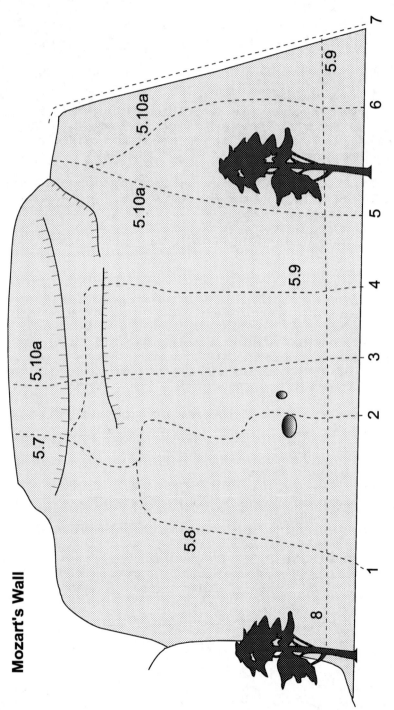

Mozart's Wall

Mozart's Wall.
This formation is tucked away in an alcove around from Beethoven's. There are several very good face climbs located here. Access to the top is from either a gully on the far left of the wall or around to the right before reaching the wall itself. There are several bolts on top; so remember to take some hangers, although a boulder and tree could be slung as an alternative. Route length 40'.

1. **FAR LEFT ROUTE*** 5.8. Follow holds to a tricky move before joining the Lefthand Route.
2. **LEFTHAND ROUTE***** 5.7. A great route with an exciting finish. Start below the big pockets and trend left to the top overhang. Getting over this is the crux.
3. **DEAD CENTER*** 5.10a. Climb straight up immediately right of the previous route, make a dyno-mantle over the overhang.
4. **CENTER ROUTE***** 5.9. A good steep wall climb with a delicate start. The crux is about 10' up. After that it's good positive holds to finish on the right to avoid the overhang, it is possible to traverse left to join the finish of the Lefthand route.
5. **AMADEUS**** 5.10a. Similar to the Center Route but the holds are smaller.
6. **AMADEUS II**** 5.10a. More face climbing fun close to the right edge.
7. **RIGHT EDGE**** 5.5. This fun slab is good for beginners.
8. **MOZART'S TRAVERSE**** 5.9. Traversing from left to right is a "foot-pump", the crux is turning the corner at the end.
THE SW EDGE*** of the boulder which forms the corridor leading to Mozart's has an overhanging boulder problem which is very good, bear hug the pin scars on the right and the edge on the left, 5.11-.

The Horned Toad.
This rock is on the left before taking the trail that leads to Mozart's; **MR TOAD'S WILD RIDE**** 5.8+ heads up the crack on the west side and over the prow. The crack on the east side leads to the prow also. There is a short route on its east face just to the left of the crack. Use nuts and one bolt stud for the anchor.

MOZART'S LEFT HAND 5.7.
The top move is compulsory.
Mark Goss climbing.

Photo by C.Owen

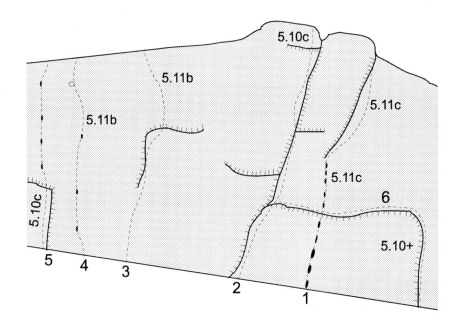

Sculpture's Crack Wall.
The routes on this overhanging wall offer very sustained strenuous climbing, mainly in old pin scars, not everyone's idea of positive holds. However the climbs are very good. There are bolt anchors at the top of the first two routes (despite the fact that natural protection is available). The other routes require sling and nut set ups. Route length 30'/40'.

1. **SAND BLAST*** 5.11c. Follow the pin scarred crack over the top; the crux is near the end. At about halfway it's possible to leave the crack and go up the face to the right. This makes it easier, cold comfort for the weak and needy.
2. **SCULPTURE'S CRACK*** 5.10c. A 3 star pump! Climb up to the corner and lieback all the way, saving some strength for the crux move over the top, which may turn out to be a belly flop if you're in any way impaired.
3. **CARLSBURG*** 5.11b. Follow an undercling flake to the right, then head straight up on very thin holds; the crux is getting over the top.
4. **SCULPTED CRACK RH*** 5.11b. Technical moves up barely adequate pin scars lead to slightly better holds. Go straight up.
5. **SCULPTED CRACK LH*** 5.10c. A problematical start leads to strenuous pin scars.
6. **SCULPTURE'S TRAVERSE*** 5.10d. From right to left. The first move is the crux; dyno from a lieback (!) then hand traverse, while drowning in a sea of lactic acid, all the way to Sculpture's Crack...and beyond if you can (harder).

The walls of Nabisco Canyon.

Opposite the easy climbs of the East Wall lie some of the hardest climbs at Stoney Point. These climbs are very overhanging and require endurance and technique. The anchors used to be the boulders in the gully behind the top; climbers are invited to continue to use these, although few can resist the convenience of clipping the bolted anchors.

Head down to the end of the canyon and go either left or right depending on which wall you wish to set up. Route length 30'/40'.

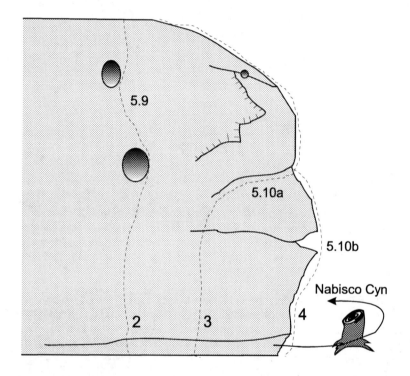

The Outside Wall of Nabisco Canyon.

1. **WALL AND SLAB** 5.9. This climb lies on the buttress to the left of the East Nabisco Wall. A wall is followed by a low angle slab which steepens towards the top. The anchor for this route consists of nut/cam placements.

2. **QUICKSILVER** 5.9+. Steep loose climbing.

3. **MERCURY** 5.10a. Up and right to a sandy traverse, then straight up the end of the buttress.

4. **WINGED MESSENGER** 5.10b. Up the overhangs at the end of the buttress.

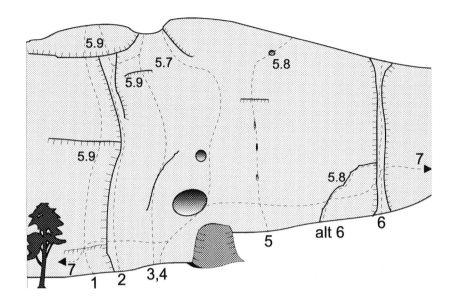

East Wall of Nabisco Canyon.
There are some very good moderate routes located on the East Wall (left as you look into the canyon). Slings and nuts make up the anchor.

1. **LEFT ROUTE*** 5.9. Climb up the overlaps to the left of the groove.
2. **EAST WALL GROOVE*** 5.7. Up the groove and, just before the overhang delicately traverse right. Going straight up over the overhang is 5.9; recommended.
3. **EAST WALL ELIMINATE*** 5.9. Uses the diagonal crack and carefully avoids bigger holds to the right and left. The crux is a mantle onto a small ledge near the top.
4. **NABISCO**** 5.7. Either start from the previous route, better, or from a boulder further up, and head up the wall, on good holds, to a ledge. The crux is the slab above.
5. **RH ROUTE**** 5.8. The steep black wall on great holds and pin scars is followed by traversing up and right on the slippery slab; crux.
6. **CHIMNEY*** 5.7. What better way to end the day? The chimney can also be gained from the left via a diagonal pin scarred crack.
7. **NABISCO TRAVERSE***** 5.11-. From left to right. A long, long voyage from strenuous hanging to thin edging, to smearing on nothing. One of Stoney's best bouldering traverses. (And it's in the shade!).

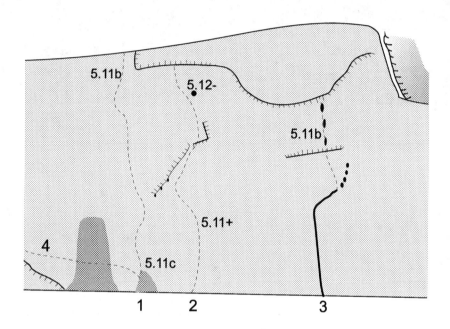

The West Wall of Nabisco Canyon.

If you want to get pumped in under 10 minutes, look no further. But get here early; these routes are popular even with beginners! Don't crank too hard on the holds as some of them are brittle. Treat these climbs with the respect that they deserve.

1. **IGUANA**** 5.11c. An undercling gains good holds (used to be better); head straight up on long reaches to a high step finish.

2. **SCURF**** 5.12. Well spaced positive holds, which get smaller every year, lead to rock which relents to merely vertical; side pulls lead to a pocket. The crux is reaching the horizontal break.

3. **MAGGIE'S FARM***** 5.11b. Some people find this route harder than the other two. A puzzling start leads to hidden holds in the crack. Follow it to the right. From here a short wall leads to the pin scars; getting past these is the crux. Great stuff!

4. **IGUANA TRAVERSE*** 5.10c. Start at Iguana but go left on large holds, the crux really needs a spot, finish at the end of the big holds, by the bush.

SKURF 5.12-.   *Photo by C.Owen*
No room for error.
Melody Wong climbing.

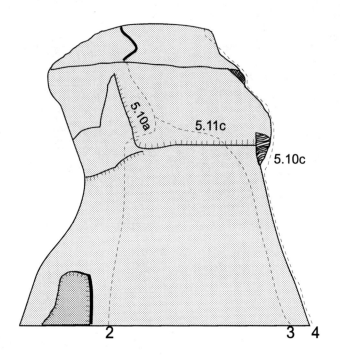

Nutcracker Buttress.
This narrow face is home to a Stoney classic. The same anchor facilitates several routes, all of them good. Use slings and nuts/cams. The easy way to the top involves heading up the canyon to the right over blocks. Route length 40'.

1. **COSMIC CORNER** 5.10d. Little is known about this route which lies left of Nutcracker.
2. **NUTCRACKER*** 5.10a. The scene of many failures, a classic. Head up on the left into an alcove, boldly step right, onto the bulge. The crux is moving up to the horizontal break. The crack above can be tricky too.
3. **NUTCRACKER DIRECT*** 5.11c. Start on the right and tackle the bulge direct on tiny holds, then join with the standard route.
4. **747*** 5.10c. Starts around the corner. Head up to the left side of the bulge and make a cruncher move onto the handhold; after this the nose of the 747 is reached. Once over the nose a fingery slab makes a fitting finale.
5. **A POCKETFUL OF TENDONITIS*** 5.10c. Slightly contrived, but good. Head up to the right, traverse right and, using pockets, climb up the steep wall to another Stoney bellyflop. Slightly loose.

NUTCRACKER CANYON TRAVERSE* 5.10/11. Start at 747 and head up and right along the canyon wall. It gets very thin.

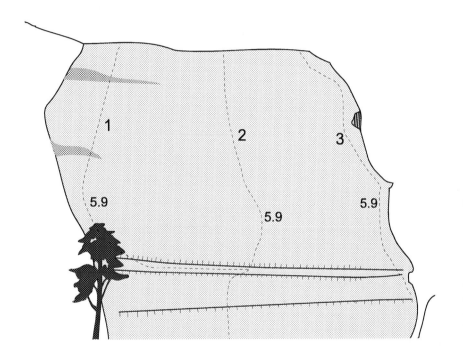

The Slab.
To reach the top of the slab head up Nutcracker Canyon, then go right. Thread belay and one bolt, take a hanger. Route length 30'.

1. **LEFT EDGE*** 5.9. Pull over the bulge then traverse left. Lieback moves lead to the top. Can be started on the left from the canyon.
2. **HEART OF GLASS*** 5.9. The same start leads to a unique problem for Stoney; a slab with potato chip edges.
3. **RIGHT EDGE*** 5.9. Step off a boulder on the right. This can also be used as an easy start for the other two routes. The crux is starting the edge.

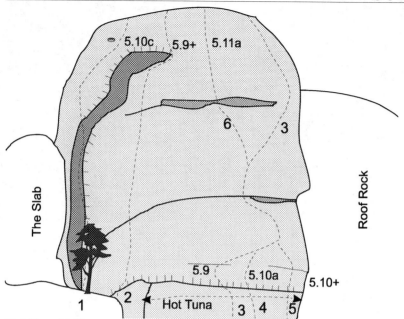

Hot Tuna Buttress.
There's some good stuff here. The anchor requires some very long slings for the tree and a #10 hex behind the boulder on the right, take two hangers for the bolts. The chimney to the left of the face provides access to the top. Route length 40'.

1. **EAT OR BE EATEN***** 5.10c. Start up the corner, then step out left onto the face. Interesting moves lead up the edge to a "why did I come?" finish.
2. **THE O-ZONE**** 5.9+. This good route has two variations, either up the corner to the overlap, or better, up the face to the right and directly up the bulge to the same place, a wild position. The crux is bypassing the overlap to the right.
3. **FLYING FISH*** 5.9. Start this climb with a jump from a boulder, the hold is big, once on the lip of Hot Tuna Roof either head up, or better, traverse right along the lip of the roof, a tough move over the second overlap leads to easy ground, finish up the rib on the right.
4. **VARIATION I*** 5.10a. It's possible to get over the lip without the jump using holds to the right.
5. **VARIATION II*** 5.10+. At the right hand end of the roof tall people can make another jump. Shorties need power and finesse (5.11a).
6. **VARIATION FINISH*** 5.11a. Go up the wall to the left of the righthand rib using small holds and pockets.
7. **COLD TURKEY*** 5.11b/c. Around to the right, in the alcove. A hard start over a bulge leads to sandy climbing up to another bulge, strenuous moves lead past this; loose holds, to easier climbing.

HOT TUNA*** V5. This Stoney classic lies beneath the Flying Fish roof, it's basically a very long and strenuous roof.

EAT OR BE EATEN 5.10c.   *Photo by C.Owen*
A technical edge.
Marc Burns climbing.

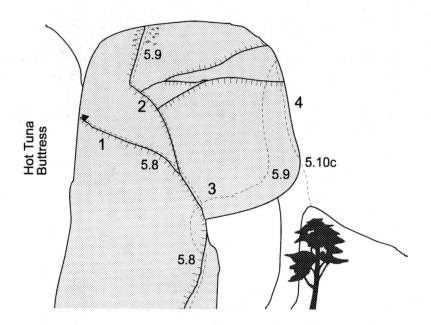

Roof Rock.
This is the last big buttress on the north side, it has seen very little traffic;
the top-rope anchor is tricky to fix, long slings are needed, a small cam placed
in a pocket near the edge helps to stop the rope from sliding over. The canyon
to the right is the way to the top. Route length 40'.

1. **LEFT CRACK*** 5.8. This crack can be led. Pass the roof using the crack on
the left and follow it all the way, past a tricky move left; be sure to finish up the
flake on the right.
2. **SANDSTORM*** 5.9. Use the same start as the previous climb but lieback up
the crack in the wall to reach pockets.
3. **FLAKESTORM**** 5.9+. A mind blower. The same crack as before; then traverse right to the edge of the wall, which is overhanging, up this quickly to a ledge,
finish up the slab above. It's a pity it's so short.
4. **STORMWARNING*** 5.10c. Starts on top of the big detached
boulder, a horizontal move, or screaming dyno, leads to good holds on the arete.
5. **LAND SHARK** 5.11b/c. Climbs up pockets on the wall around the corner.
6. **THE SHARK'S TOOTH** 5.10b/c. Lies to the right of the previous route.

THE O~ZONE 5.9+.   *Photo by C.Owen*
At bulge #1.
Terry Wasson-Graf climbing.

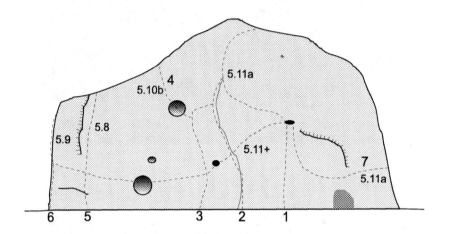

Carousel Rock ~ North East Side.
There are some good thin face climbs on this boulder. The easiest way up is a 5.8 on the south side, the holds are a little loose, there are bolts on top so take some hangers. Route length 30'.

1. **THE ROLLERCOASTER**** 5.10d/5.11a. Gain the pocket and traverse to the left, getting on the small ledge is the crux and can prove quite baffling, finish up the very thin face.
2. **VARIATION START**** 5.11a. Start left of the previous route and head up the rib to a ledge, one more move reaches the previous route at the baffling crux.
3. **VARIATION START II** 5.10d. Start left of the rib, climb straight up to a pocket then step right and onto the baffling crux ledge.
4. **SANCTUARY** 5.10b. Same start as Var.II but go left and finish up the tricky wall.
5. **CAROUSEL FACE*** 5.8. The left side of the face using large holds.
6. **CAROUSEL EDGE*** 5.9. Dyno up the overhanging arete.
7. **TRAVERSE OF CAROUSEL ROCK***** V4. Ironically, the best long hard boulder traverse at Stoney lies far from the madding crowd - only ghosts with chalk climb this route. Thin slabs, thin edges, dynos; the works...

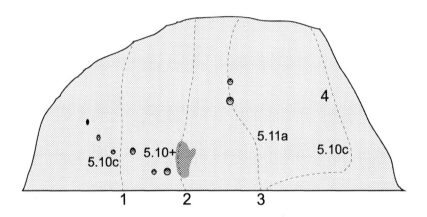

Slanderland ~ North Side.
Getting to the top is a real adventure! If you're really good at bouldering, you can solo to the top at the south east end; otherwise throwing a rope over the top then going up the slab works. There is a bolt with a hanger on top, take a kevlar prussik loop to thread the hole. For a back up a long sling tied to a tree on the ground helps. Route length 35'.

North Face.
1. **REGGAE ROUTE**** 5.10b/c. A problematical start on chopped holds leads to the crux, a delicate move; after this it's easier.
2. **HOLY *?!#**** 5.10d. Up and left to a steep section, technical and delicate moves lead to easier stuff. One of Stoney's hardest slabs.
3. **THE 5.10 SLAB*** 5.11a. Another hard slab on very indefinite holds.
4. **THE 5.9 SLAB**** 5.10c. Traverse right to the edge; tricky, even trickier moves lead up past the bolt stud to easier ground.

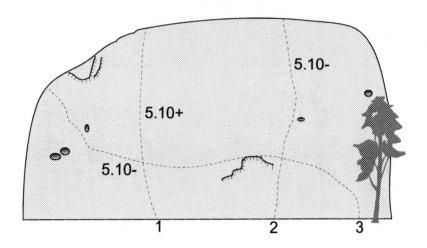

Slanderland II ~ South Side.
Located just north of the previous boulder, the easiest way up is to solo up the chopped holds on the north side. Bolt anchors on top; take hangers. Route length 30'

1. **ROUTE RUSTLIN'*** 5.10+. The steep climb on the left.
2. **YARD THE TOOL*** 5.10a/b. Steep with a tricky finish.
3. **ALICE IN SLANDERLAND**** 5.10a. From the tree around to the NE corner. At the chopped holds on the north side go down. What it lacks in difficulty it makes up with character. *Use a spotter.*

To the north of Stoney Point is a small outcropping; there is a beautiful lieback crack located here;
FREEWAY CRACK (AKA THE GIFT)***5.9+, this strenuous route can be led.

The longest routes at Stoney Point are located on these walls, and although they include some excellent face climbs, there is not much activity here, even on weekends; because of this lack of traffic there are some loose holds; treat the climbs with care.

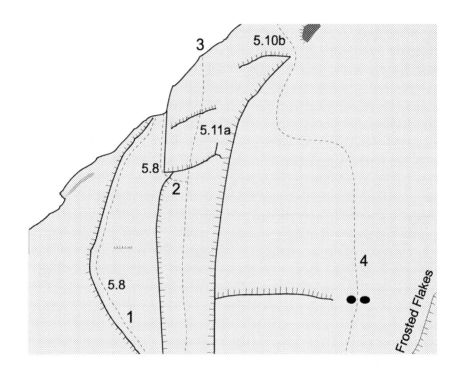

Suburbia Wall ~ Left Side.
This is located close to the north west corner, the top can be gained by going around the corner to the left, cross a slab and head up a gully and step over a crevasse. Very long slings are required for the anchors. Route length 45'.

1. **LEFTHAND CRACK*** 5.8. Follow the ramp left and finish up the crack, or better, traverse right along an undercling to finish.
2. **PEDESTAL CRACK*** 5.8. Climb to the top of The Pedestal a tricky step left leads to the exposed crack.
3. **KAIRO*** 5.10d/5.11a. From the top of The Pedestal the wall above can be overcome using an off balance mantle.
4. **NORTHWEST PASSAGE*** 5.10b. A good steep face leads to the overhang, the crux is getting over this section.

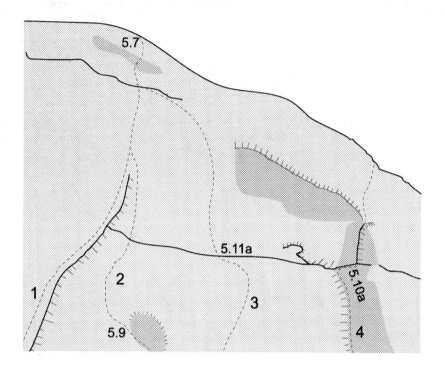

Suburbia Wall ~ Right Side.

1. **FROSTED FLAKES***** 5.7. A good moderate route up the black section of rock, the finish is the crux; a fiendish mantle.
2. **TONY THE TIGER**** 5.9. Starts just right of the previous route. Climb up bulging rock on good holds, eventually joining Frosted Flakes.
3. **CIRCUS GAMES*** 5.11a. Climb the steep wall using pockets and flakes, getting past the overhang is the crux.
4. **SWEET SUBURBIA**** 5.10a. An intimidating route. Climb up the rotten corner then make a committing traverse right, lieback up the overhanging crack and climb the wall above on dubious holds.

The face to the left of Suburbia Wall has some interesting short top rope problems, 5.7/5.8. There are also some top rope routes located in the crevasse encountered during the approach to the top. Both walls have been climbed; the routes range from 5.7 on the left to 5.11 on the righthand wall. However, this place smells of guano and has a lot of trash.

A-FRAME RIGHT 5.9.   *Photo by C.Owen*
Let the games begin...
Chris Savage climbing.

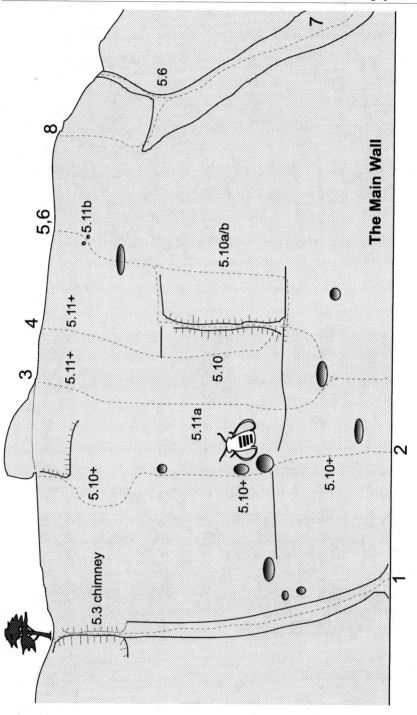

The Main Wall

5.3 chimney

5.10+

5.11+

5.11+

5.10+

5.11a

5.10+

5.10

5.11b

5.10a/b

5,6

8

5.6

7

3

4

1

2

The Main Wall.
This is the highest piece of rock at Stoney Point. The steep face makes for some thrilling climbs. To reach the top; either solo up the S-Crack or go up the broken buttress to the right (the same approach as The Jesus Wall and The Pillar). Long slings and nuts/cams make up the anchors. Use a 165' rope. Route length 80'.

1. **S-CRACK***** 5.3. An excellent beginners route on the left margin of the wall. The crux is the chimney at the top. Usually led.
2. **KILLER BEES*** 5.10+"bee". Do this one on a cold morning, when the bees aren't so angry! Start to the right of S-Crack at a small round pocket. Climb up into a scoop and make a weird mantle, the first crux, the rock is loose but stick with it because it improves higher up, gain the ledge by the bees nest and climb the slightly overhanging wall to the left of it; the second crux. The next section is easier and a Thank God ledge provides a welcome rest, traverse left along this and step onto a foothold which leads to an undercling, the third crux involves gaining the blank slab, easier climbing leads past the corner to the top.
3. **MAIN WALL**** 5.11+. The next four routes tackle the wall and share the same start. Using pockets and flakes gain the scoop; good, hard, face climbing leads up this over a slight bulge to a ledge. The pocketed face above starts out well but becomes an exercise in very thin face climbing (crux).
4. **I HAVE FAITH**** 5.11+. Start in the same place as the previous climb but head right aiming for a ledge at the bottom of the obvious vee groove. Step out left onto the wall and in a great position head straight up, then trend right for the crux finish on sloping pockets.
5. **PICK POCKET*** 5.11b. From the groove ledge; up this then traverse right to a good ledge beneath another pocketed face, leaving the last two pockets is the crux.
6. **OZYMANDIAS***** 5.11b. An awesome wall climb. From the vee groove ledge steep exposed climbing (5.10a/b) leads up the black face to the right. The crux is the same finish as Pick Pocket.
7. **THE MAIN CHIMNEY*** 5.6. Up the dihedral and over the bulge, much easier climbing leads to the crux; up and right over a little wall to gain the slab above. This is a lead.
8. **VARIATION FINISH** 5.11. Instead of going right at the little wall, go to the left of the overhang and finish up using pockets.

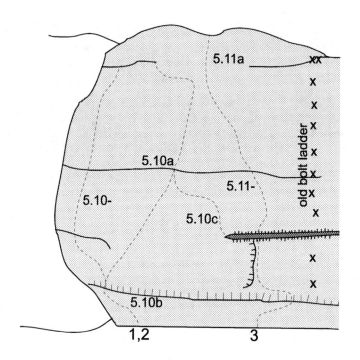

The Jesus Wall ~ Left Side.

This wall is not quite as steep as The Main Wall. The holds are smaller however and the routes are long, delicate and exposed. Approach the top from the right, up the broken buttress and the tricky little wall, then go to the left; a tree, slings, nuts and cams make up the anchor. Route length 70'.

1. **LEFT EDGE**** 5.10b. Strenuous moves over the overhang lead to face climbing up the left edge of the wall. Finish by traversing left into the top of Main Chimney.

2. **JESUS WALL LEFT***** 5.10c. The same start as the previous climb but trend right and up the depression in the wall, great moves lead up this to the final headwall; traverse left to finish up the arete or finish up the following route.

3. **CENTRAL ROUTE***** 5.11a. A delicate climb just to the left of the old bolt ladder. Mantle onto a ledge then go left to a crack, this leads to a ledge (possible to toe traverse left to join Jesus Wall Left from here, a good variation) from here go up and right then straight up to the crux headwall, bouldering moves lead to a sandy crack and then the top. Fantastic!!

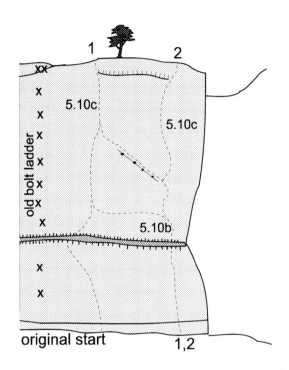

The Jesus Wall ~ Right Side.

1. **JESUS WALL***** 5.10c. This climb has changed over the years; it used to go up just right of the old bolt ladder. Missing holds have made this more difficult and the climb is usually started on the right side of the wall; from a ledge above the overlap either traverse left to reach better holds or head up to reach a diagonal line of pockets, follow these left and finish up the wall above on dubious holds.

2. **CRUCIFIX**** 5.10b/c. A variation finish. Instead of going left using the pockets; go straight up on loose holds; a little steeper.

3. **THE CRACK** 5.8. A nasty hand crack.

4. **LITTLE JESUS*** 5.9/5.10a. Climbs the wall to the right of the crack.

JESUS WALL RIGHT 5.10c.
Lonely, technical and thin.
Noreen Flynn climbing.

Photo by C.Owen

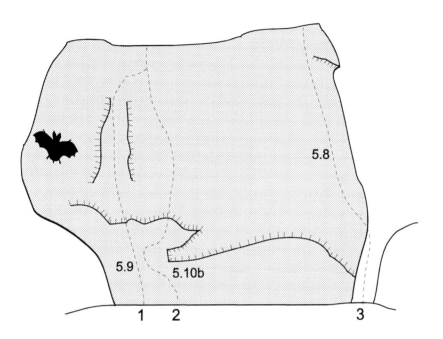

Bat Boulder.
So called because of the red bat painted on its east face. A jump from a boulder
to the south leads to the top, take slings and nuts/cams for the anchor. Route
length 30'.

1. **THE BAT*** 5.9. An overhanging start; the crux, leads to moves to exit the
alcove then easier climbing.
2. **NEVER SAY DIE**** 5.10b. An even tougher overhanging start leads   to steep
face climbing on good holds.
3. **J.T.*** 5.8. The slab on the right by a couple of variations.
4. **LUCY** 5.8. Straight up the west face, tricky start; loose.

Boulder Problems:
CRACK 5.8+. A short crack lies just in the cave, jamming up pinscars.

Skull Rock

The top can be reached by swinging over the lip as seen from the top of Mommy's Boys.

1. **WEST FACE*** 5.9. The steep face with some variations.
2. **THE SKULL** 5.10+. Up to the pockets, then strenuous moves up and right.
3. **EASY FACE*** 5.4. Another way to the top.

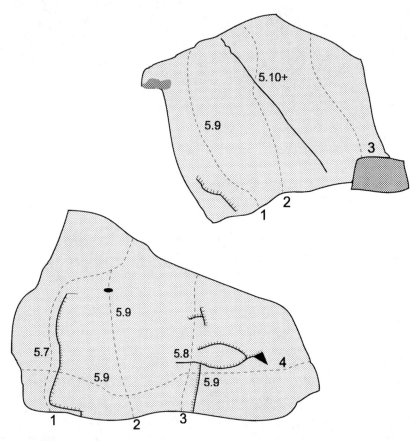

Mommy's Boys ~ North Face.

This boulder is unusual because it lies perpendicular to the bed-plane of Stoney Point, traditional roof flakes have become face flakes, which makes it a good spot for climbing something different. Beginners should use a tope rope, there are 2 bolt studs up on top.

1. **LEFT ROUTE*** 5.7. A tricky start leads to a lieback flake, then go right, or straight up. A little loose.
2. **THE FACE**** 5.9. Fun delicate moves up chopped holds.
3. **RIGHT ROUTE*** 5.8. A high step start leads to sharp in-cut edging.
4. **MOMMY'S TRAVERSE*** 5.9. From right to left, thin smedging.

5.0
Slab (Slant Rock)
Stairs*
5.1
East Face Route*(Boulder 1)
5.2
Edge
Jam Crack*
West face
5.3
Not Another One
S-Crack***
Split Rock Chimney**
5.4
Beehive***
Easy Face (Skull)
5.5
Arch Chimney
Chockstone Chimney
Pin Scars Chimney
Right Edge**
Spencer's Slab Left**
5.6
Left Slab Route*
Main Chimney*
Nose*
Potholes*(Turlock)
Ramada*
Scarface*
Slab** (Slab Rock)
Vivarin*
5.7
Beethoven's Crack**
Black's Crack**
Body Chute
Chatsworth Chimney
Chimney*
Crown of Thorns**
East Wall Groove*
Flake***
Flaky Crack*
Frosted Flakes***
Left Hand Route***(Mozart's)
Left Route*(Mommy's)
Lieback Flake*
Mantle Start**
Nabisco**
North Face*
North Flake*
North Side LH

Overhang Passby*
Potholes Escape**
Short Story**
Untold Story*
5.8
Carousel Face*
Crack(Jesus Wall)
Crack(Pillar)
Easy Route*
Face*(Jam Rock)
Far Left*
J.T.*
Left Crack*(Roof Rock)
LH Crack*(Suburbia)
Lucy
Pedestal Crack*
RH Crack
RH Route**
Right Route*(Mommy's)
Right Slab Route*
Riddler**
Slab Route (Lower Tier)
Slot
Studley Slab
5.8+
Crack (Bat)
Mr Toad's Wild Ride**
5.9
A-Frame Right***
Bat*
Black Crack*
Bracket*
Carousel Edge*
Center Route***
Chouinard's Slab*
Composure***
Connections*
Dihedral Left
Dihedral Right
E.Wall Eliminate*
Easy Money
Face**(Mommy's)
Flying Fish*
Front Route
Heart of Glass*
Left Edge*
Left Route*(Nab.Wall)
Magnum Case*
Mantles (Slant)
Mommy's Traverse*
Mozart's Traverse**

Now Voyager
Paul's Hole***
Pillar Left*
Pillar Right*
Pin Scars*(Tur.)
Pin Scars***
Pink Drips RH*
Pink Drips***
Potholes Crack*
Potholes**
Right Edge*
Sandstorm*
Tierdrop*
Tony the Tiger**
Turlock Face*
Wall and Slab
West Face Skull

5.9+
Borealis
Flakestorm**
Johnny Cat*
Left Route(Swiss)
Nose Eliminate**
O-Zone**
Quicksilver
Red Dawn*
Right Route*(Swiss)
Slab & Crack
Todd's Traverse***

5.10a
Alice in Slanderland**
Amadeus II**
Amadeus**
Aurora*
Bolted Lead
Center Route**
Chockstone Wall
Corner (B1)
Dead Center*
Hog Tied*
Left Arete*
Little Jesus*
Mercury
Mugnesea Lung**
North Side RH
Nutcracker***
Offset Slab*
Pocket Rocket*
Savage Slab**
Slab Traverse**
Smedge**

Spencer's RH*
Sweet Suburbia**
Tidy Cat*
Variation I*

5.10b
A-Frame Left
Left Edge**
Never Say Die**
NW Passage**
Overlord*
Pink Drips Direct**
Preying Mantis*
Sanctuary
Telephone Booth
Three Pigs*
Underworld**
Winged Messenger
Yard the Tool*

5.10c
5.9 Slab**
747***
Arete Skeleton
Black Roof*
Black Wall***
Bull Market*
Crucifix**
Direct**(Beet's)
Eat or be Eaten***
Eye of Faith***
Hoof and Mouth***
Iguana Traverse*
Jesus Wall Left***
Jesus Wall***
Mantlepeace*
Owl Hole*
Pocket of Tendonitis*
Rabbits Foot*
Reggae Route**
Sculpted Crack LH*
Sculpture's Crack***
Sharkstooth
Stormwarning*
Undercling

5.10d
Changeling**
Cosmic Corner
Holy Shit**
Split Decision*
Wounded Knee**
Wrath of Kahan*

5.10+
10-40
Bird Hole*
Bulge
East Face (Pile Ups)
Killer Bees**
Potholes Traverse***
Rainbow's End**
Route Rustlin'*
Sculpture's Traverse***
Skull
Spiral Traverse***
Variation II Flying Fish*
Middle Route
5.11a
5.10 Slab*
Batman & Owen*
Beegone*
Boot Flake**
Captain Energy*
Central Route**
Circus Games*
Corner*
Corner the Market**
Kairo*
Layed Off*
Left Edge**
Lip Traverse**
Mantis Mantel
Nabisco Traverse***
Packer Cracker
Pliers*
Prow Var.**
Prow***
Pump Traverse**
Rollercoaster**
Slime*
SW Edge***
Spiral Traverse***
Turlock Eliminate*
Var.Finish Flying Fish*
5.11b
Black Friday*
Carlsburg*
Maggie's Farm***
Ozymandias***
Pebble Traverse
Pick Pocket*
Sculpted Crack RH*
SE Corner*(B1)

5.11c
Cold Turkey*
Iguana**
Landshark
Nutcracker Dir.***
Sandblast**
5.11
Black Friday*
Crowd Pleaser**
Eat Out More Often*
Nutcracker Traverse*
Nylon Boy*
Pile Up Mantle
Right Route
South Face (Pile Ups)
5.11+
Black Monday*
Crack* (B1)
Crystal Ball Mantle**
Ear*
Edge* (B1)
Endo Boy*
I Have Faith**
Left Edge**
Main Wall**
Pile Driver**
Pink Floyd*
Right Route
Scrambled Eggs Traverse*
Semidetached**
Slant Rock Traverse*
Sledgehammer*
5.12
Dart Lady
Dynomite**
Plank
Skurf***
Vicious***
V's
Carousel Rock Traverse*** V4
Cranking Queenie** V3
Expansion Chamber*** V5
Hot Tuna*** V5
Master of Reality** V5
Pile Lieback* V4
Power Glide** V4
Traverse of Bold.1* V4
Traverse of Turlock** V5
Vaino's Dyno** V5

Front Cover Shot,
The O-Zone,
Noreen Flynn climbing.

Rear Cover Shot,
A Study of Canyon Boulder.

by C.Owen

rock shoe

RESOLING
SPECIALIST

- 2-3 DAY SHOP TIME
- ALL BRANDS OF RUBBER
- FULL WARRANTY

Half Soles: $30.00/pr
Rand Repair: $8.00/ea shoe
Return Mail: $3.00/pr
Call for other repair costs

Mail shoes along with check or M.O. or come by, there's a drop off box on the porch, in case we are out.

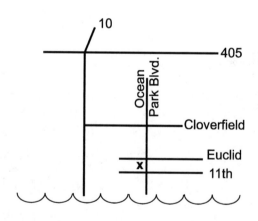

1201 Ocean Park Blvd. #A
Santa Monica, CA 90405.
(310) 452-2346 'till 10:00PM.

WANTED: SERIOUS CLIMBERS!

L.A. Rock Gym
4926 W. Rosecrans Avenue
Hawthorne, CA 90250
(310) 973-3388

L.A. ROCK GYM

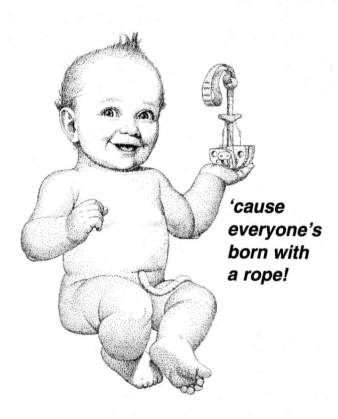

the ACCESS FUND

...preserving America's diverse climbing resources.

The Access Fund, a national, non-profit climbers' organization, is working to keep you climbing. The Access Fund works to preserve access and protect the environment by buying land, funding climber-support facilities, financing scientific studies, helping develop land management policy, publishing educational materials, and providing resources to local climbers' coalitions.

Every climber can help preserve access!

Commit yourself to "leaving no trace."
Remove litter, old slings, etc., from crags and the base of walls.

Dispose of human waste properly.
Use toilets whenever possible. If none are available, dig a six-inch deep hole at least 160 feet from water and bury waste. Always pack out toilet paper (use zip-lock plastic bags).

Use existing trails.
Avoid cutting switchbacks and trampling vegetation.

Use discretion when placing bolts & fixed protection.
Camouflage all anchors. Bolting above public trails is discouraged.

Respect restrictions to protect natural resources and cultural artifacts.
Be aware of seasonal closures to protect nesting raptors.
Power drills are illegal in wilderness areas.
Never manufacture holds in natural rock.
No other activity so seriously threatens climbers' access.

Park in designated areas.
Try not to park in undeveloped, vegetated areas.

Maintain a low profile.

Respect private property.
Consult landowners before developing new crags.

Join or form a local group to deal with access issues.

Join the Access Fund.
To become a member, make a tax-deductible donation of any amount.

The Access Fund - PO Box 17010 - Boulder, CO 80308

"Yet every world should have one unclimbable mountain."

Larry Niven
Ringworld